DEMON POND

BY CHRISTOPHER DEWDNEY

POETRY

Golders Green 1971
A Palaeozoic Geology of London, Ontario 1973
Fovea Centralis 1975
Alter Sublime 1980
Predators of the Adoration 1983
Permugenesis 1987
The Radiant Inventory 1988
Demon Pond 1994

NON-FICTION

The Immaculate Perception 1986
The Secular Grail 1993

Demon Pond

poems by

Christopher Dewdney

M&S

Canadian Cataloguing in Publication Data

Dewdney, Christopher, 1951-
Demon pond

ISBN 0-7710-2693-5

I. Title.

PS8557.E846D4 1994 C811'.54 C94.930404-2
PR9199.3.D48D4 1994

The publishers acknowledge the support of the Canada
Council, the Ontario Arts Council, and the Ontario
Ministry of Culture, Tourism and Recreation for their
publishing program.

The poems "The Beach" and "The Woman"
utilize found material.

The author wishes to thank Stan Dragland and
Barbara Gowdy for their assistance.

Typeset in Goudy by M&S, Toronto

Printed and bound in Canada on acid-free paper.

McClelland & Stewart Inc.
The Canadian Publishers
481 University Avenue
Toronto, Ontario
M5G 2E9

1 2 3 4 5   98 97 96 95 94

CONTENTS

THE GLASS MACHINE

The Empty Sunlight 3

Poem Begun with a Line from a Dream 4

The Birch Leaves 5

New Moon in July 6

The Lynx in the Rapids 7

Haiku 8

Windhover 9

Rain Haiku 11

Time Travel 12

The Pines 14

Ghost Catchers 16

Ring of Shadows 17

The Fossil Forest of Axel Heiberg 18

Wind Angels 20

Demon Pond 22

Ghostwalker 24

The Watchers by the Pond 25

Imago 27

Wind Walker 28

The Clouds 29

November 31

Winter Solstice 33

At the Department Store 35

Winter Hawk 36

Orion 2.7° K 37

ARTIFACTS OF SILENCE

White Sands	41
Train Song	44
The World Poem	45
Night Wind	47
Litany	49
Hollow Wind, Empty Stars	52
Monkey Light	53
Norge Union	54
The Blue Windy Day	55
M95ED	57
The Beach	58
Language	61
The Woman	62
H26L3	63
Seven Electrical Angels	64
Idea	66
H10B7	67
Line gauge	68
K37Y9	69

DEMON POND

The Glass Machine

*The ragged sparks blew down the wind. The prairie
about them lay silent. Beyond the fire was the cold and
the night was clear and the stars were falling. The old
hunter pulled his blanket about him. I wonder if there's
other worlds like this, he said. Or if this is the only one.*

CORMAC MC CARTHY

A field of roses
impossible in the March
sunlight. Our faces
hallucinatory with love.
Cellular tides
in the gravity of total permission.
Our hearts
a shadow play against
drawn blinds. And our smiles
synchronous with the speed
of just being here
are perfectly honest,
ebbing and waxing in accord
with the spontaneous harmony
of our internal light.
The continuous transformation
of our identity.

This sunny day
we are chiaroscuro,
inhabitants of a white room
whose flickering interior
is a temporal piebald
of light and dark.
Trace the passage
of those quick ragged clouds
over the sun.

The windows of your shutters halfway down
cried to me the life of the child.
You are not so old
that you cannot lie naked
in the autumn leaves.
Even now, in such raw spring
as conjoins the end of winter
with the first flowers
we speak of the dread pools.
For the sun is a windy object
and its poetry free of device.
In my mind the leaves
have already opened.

You are dreaming a dream you've dreamt many
times, and in this dream you are in a place you've
visited many times in your dreams. Imagine that this
place, with which you are so familiar, is a forgotten
parallel life, so real your daily existence becomes a
vanishing memory lost in its depths. Then imagine
this dream illuminated by full waking consciousness,
the monochromatic light of the unconscious
suddenly transformed, exalted, by Technicolor, by
depth. The birch leaves turning in the late evening
sun, wagging greenly in the summer wind.

Imagine moving in this dream. The softness of
the wind, the odour of it in your nostrils. Surveying
the world in a panorama of hallucinogenic clarity
you look behind you and discover that you are
standing in front of someone. And you turn and
look to see yourself turning and looking at someone
turning and looking at yourself turning and looking
at yourself.

Apart
for exactly
one lunar cycle.
Summer hardening
into the full mystery
of our love. Leaves
in the night wind.
Supernatural, love
my heart flies to you
along a burning axis
of vision. Skimming
the surface
of these dark northern lakes.

Pale splendour
of the new moon.
Its magic twofold
by that measure
we each know
the world.

It is a grey, rainless summer afternoon. You are walking through a northern hardwood forest beside a river. You hear a baby crying from the brush near the rapids. As you approach the sound, the hairs on the nape of your neck prick up. You step onto a rocky clearing beside the rapids. A wet lynx sits on the flat rock verging the cataract, its back to you.

The lynx turns its head to look at you over its shoulder. Its eyes are almost entirely pupil, the thin rim of an elliptical, gold iris barely visible around the black crystal caverns of its pupils. You have stood here before. In memory you scream magnetically as you pluck the irises from your own eyes in a mirror. The iris-tissue like gold foil slipping off pupils that are dark openings onto an unknowable, alien emptiness. The sirens begin to wail. You turn to run as the world starts to break up. The lynx wheels and leaps in one bound onto your shoulders, sinking its teeth into the back of your head. You are drawn whole into the black vacuum of the lynx's mouth. The lynx transforms into an enormous horned serpent, its body containing a universe of stars.

The world is a prison that has shrunk to the outline of your body. You are now free to move.

A gentle breeze
moves the leaves, harms
nothing.

The cold front that blew in overnight was still restless as we made our way into the field. Washed by yesterday's rain and dried in the wind under nameless stars, the air had become quick and optical. Single leaves on the forested slopes of the valley were visible across the fields. Through this lucid æther the sunlight accelerated unimpeded, tempering the unseasonably cool summer morning. The birds were silent, as if rapt in the hush of some greater music.

The strong winds of the previous night had moved on like an army, leaving marauding gusts to roam the summer landscape in loose formations. Each one a billowing, constantly involuting entity that surged and ebbed, swooping from invisible quarters of the sky. Some gusts combined and then separated, others blew themselves out into the particularities of a woodlot and dissipated in a school of zephyrs.

The wind spawned smaller eddies and vortices – these were discrete and capricious. They insinuated themselves into the hollows of old trees. They vanished into the reeds by the creek, and like unseen waterstriders engraved brief darts on the surface of the stream.

Between gusts there was a granular silence complicated by the continuous, distant clamour of the wind. As we walked through the bright grass a strong downdraught spilled noisily over the crowns of some large maples nearby. Then, as abruptly as the deluge had started, it stopped. The maple branches rebounded in sudden weightlessness. The air around us was still until a tributary from the same cascade drenched the field beside us, flattening the hissing grass. Then it was roaring in our ears, snapping our clothing against our skin. When the gust moved on, its progress unmarked, everything became still again in the dusty silence. The gale, which had moved the maples and flooded the field, was invisible until it swept through the soughing combs of a white pine on the far ridge. Even this sound was amplified, an aural homologue of the air's transparency.

A single kestrel plied the wind above our heads. Dipping and hovering like a panoptic, predatory kite, it stalked its own shadow flickering insubstantial through the grass.

RAIN HAIKU

A wet grey day
warm carnival wind
blowing through my soul.

Before she left she ate an apple and an orange. The apple core and orange peels she clumped atop a white porcelain plate on the wooden dining table beside the kitchen door. It was night, she'd be out for an hour or so left the light on for her husband who would be home soon. She would do the dishes when she returned, perhaps he would wash them before then.

Later that evening she came back to find the kitchen door ajar. Called his name he didn't answer, he hadn't come home yet working late. She didn't remember leaving the door open, though she must have. A few moths had gathered around the porch light in the early evening darkness. On the table the orange peels visibly drier and the apple core brown, as if in her absence some force had been through the house delicately altering everything.

The dishes in the sink contained the same, shallow pools of dishwater the passage of time subtle there. The light in the kitchen exactly the same, the vibrations of the filament unnoticed though brighter because darker outside. A force had flowed through the house needed no point of entry everything a sieve to time's particulate and invisible touch. She hadn't come home to the same room never would again.

Her husband's steps on the stairs to the porch before his hand on the handle of the screen door

pulling it open the first glimpse of his smile the time-
wind slower there. The subtle opening to time
behind now they sit down and he peels a fresh
orange.

White was the colour farthest
behind the pines,
above all the colours
you spoke of that afternoon.
And the green pines were like
pictures of themselves
taken from inside the sun.
And remembering our words
you were sad later in the evening.

And now this colourless black,
signifying what, unreasoned,
cannot be undone.
Does it sing for you
when you stand alone,
when you pose for an
invisible camera to
allay the cool, reasoned violence
of this world? Black
was the possibility of all colours.

But that was before
your sadness became the measure
of such pale, articulate darkness as
you now navigate.
Before your song echoed

within the tragic hills.
Your song of white.
White sailing on white,
on white declined.

The evening before our departure the weather turns. A brooding wind rises as the skies darken with clouds, hastening the late-summer twilight of northern Ontario. The wind heralds a change of seasons and the foliage is restless with it. Its urgency stirs migratory birds in their roosts.

The north-end cabin is a warm refuge, though beginning to empty in anticipation of our absence. The whole island, as well as the forest on the far shore of the lake, seems already deserted, vacant of our voices and gestures.

Our imminent departure creates a premonitory nostalgia. The ghosts of our summer idyll are blowing invisibly through the trees on the island, catching in the twigs and leaves before being pulled away. The black spruce and birch are spirit catchers. They snag shreds of our souls, filaments that will drift to earth some hollow, sunny autumn afternoon.

But on this late August evening we haunt the landscape. The leaves are alive with our gestures. Animated by the dark wind, the trees imitate us to hold our presence. Small human flames in the winter to come.

I am a ring of shadows
around you. As if
you were a tall shining thing
rising before me,
a quavering, unearthly shape.
Unnatural clarity
of your face I
know you
are love.

Some forty-five million years ago, the earth's climate was so mild that the Arctic regions had a sub-tropical climate. Axel Heiberg, a large island in the Canadian Arctic, was the site of a lush forest of Dawn Redwoods and palmettos. It is thought that deciduous trees first acquired their habit of shedding their leaves in these Eocene Arctic forests, for summer nights lasted five months.

The Arctic Eocene forest rises from the floor of a vast, dark library. The deserted wing of a Georgian museum. Its ceiling beams cannot be seen above the stars, nor are the walls visible beyond the horizon. During the long, still months of the Arctic night meteoric dust falls from the sky. It powders the leaves of the forest like the leaves of untended lobby plants in a vacant apartment building. On the forest floor vaguely coloured shadows flicker weirdly under the aurora borealis. The leaves above are waxen, shining dustily iridescent.

Lemurs glide through the stillness – silent, quick hallucinations. Their claws rustle on the thin, ribboned bark of the Dawn Redwoods. They are the only movement in this inconceivable atrium, this sub-tropical, polar forest of perpetual twilight.

The soft, feathery needles of the Dawn Redwoods – their ginkgo silhouettes in the perpetual gloom of an endless summer night.

The Eocene Arctic forest is a hiatus in time

where abandoned lovers return to the arms of their
beloved. It is where secrets are kept, a lonely place of
solitary wandering. It is the arena of love gone
vacant, of heartbroken lovers deserted by mad
partners. A zone of silent, strange encounters –
luminescent mushroom gardens fluttering with giant
tropical moths. And when the wind comes, soft at
first, then rushing, spreading through the night
forest, the first chords of the great Nachtmusik are
written.

And the chill rain, sometimes for weeks.

We are waiting
at the line between
today and tomorrow, night
and day. The planetary
terminator line, stalled
in perpetual twilight
early in the Arctic Eocene night.

In the continuous flux of the world,
in its debris, I pronounce the ritual names.
The Eocene terminator line
holds us in its dusky thrall
as the mists of a forty-million-
year-old forest
rise again to the canopy.

A strong wind had blown steadily for two days. The gusts moaned in the balustrade of our balcony, which faced south and overlooked the ocean. It was on the railings of this balcony that the first angels appeared on the evening of the second day, just as migratory birds, blown off course into the open sea, fall exhausted onto the decks of ships.

By nightfall there were seven of them, between five and eight inches in length, facing the wind with their wings folded back. You could see them scrabbling for purchase against the buffeting of unusually strong gusts. Periodically throughout that evening we shone a flashlight out of the kitchen window to make sure they were still there. I remember the way the beam caught the facets of their wings in the darkness.

The wind died overnight, and at first light the next morning they were gone. The balcony was as empty as if they'd never been there at all.

Some several days later my wife confessed that she'd had strangely lucid dreams the night of the angels and that since then she'd been hearing a silent, inner music, which had only now begun to fade. I was shocked to hear her description, for I had experienced exactly the same sensations. The music, almost indistinguishable from the background of inner thoughts, had started during my lucid dreams. It had a chiming, ineffable clarity impossible to reproduce.

Whenever it is sunny and windy now, we both glance at the deck, hoping to see an angel flattening itself in the lee of a newel post or on a railing near the corner. They have never returned. We know now that there are two winds – one blows through the visible world, and one blows through our hearts. Even though the angels have never reappeared, we have both heard the music, faintly, as they migrate through windy nights.

You step into the crucible,
the philosophical egg, vessel
of the sun and moon. The surface
of this liquid
intersects your thigh
like a bracelet
of exaltation. Matter itself
ringing out a single
clear note.

You step into the water,
indigenous, exquisite.
Your quick grace alive
wire, eerie where I falter
in sweet sickness.
Stirring up the dreams
at the bottom of the pond.
Every gesture, the most incidental
of your movements is slender,
candid. You are perfection
doubled back on itself,
standing before me in this
labyrinthine night forest,
a cool autumn mist
over the water.

Our union is a confederacy
outside the common world.

Each other the most remarkable
being we've ever met, adored
by the adored.
The one for whom
we had abandoned hope
years before.
My mind goes anywhere
my hands and mouth travel
weightless and eager
over your radiant flesh.
Snakes aroused by humans coupling
and hallucinations of unearthly paradise
rise like ghostly moths
to the light we burn by.
Hosts of invisible beings
lap at the fiery column
that is us. Flesh a distraction
on our way to a deeper union.

Your love, your body
the knife that cut me
open to my bliss.

You are
unnatural. I have
never seen a being
shine this brightly
from her eyes.
To have you step so lightly
beside me is a joy the
clear intensity
of your skin. As if
you were some
Apsana incarnate,
a vision, the sign
of completion. The terminus
of this perceptual feast.

Heaven's undoing
your hair the stars' keep.

The smell of time-travel lingers in dusty attics, in basement storage rooms lit by a single light bulb, in the corners of unused closets. Within these sealed chambers, months, even years, may elapse between visits. Collections of partially abandoned articles register the gestures and energy of those who placed them here. In these rooms these things will remain unchanged as all else changes, as lives change, as children become adults and friends move away.

It is here, on an errand to recover camping equipment, or Christmas decorations, you smell the scent of the time-travellers. Perhaps they have just closed the door, their redolence lingering as a woman's perfume persists in a room she has left. They are those unchanging few who are free of gradual transformation and decline. Their scent arouses you the way the smell of jet-fuel excites a traveller bound for exotic shores.

By the edge of the autumn pond the watchers begin to materialize in the twilight. Under the darkening sky you see that her face is older now, your love even more vulnerable, more apparent as you age. You turn and walk down the basement stairs and open the wooden door of the storage room. Flicking on the light you notice a dry smell, an old smell, then something else. The time-travellers have been here. An eddy of air they stirred has yet to settle in the corner of the room. And then you realize it was you yourself who had just been here, a second earlier, a year earlier, a little younger, a little more hopeful.

Fathomless, still October night.
Cool, deep moonlight on the trees. Silence.
And the leaves are dropping tonight.
Windless, chill evening
in the deserted forest of
maple and oak and the leaves
are falling,
falling almost weightless,
like bats fluttering down
     a great shedding,
     a settling.
The dark canopy rustling, disintegrating,
collapsing piecemeal. The leaves are stemmed ærofoils
drifting to earth.

Full moon and the trees are
losing their leaves tonight.
Summer's scales
peeling.

At night the autumn wind animates the dry oak
leaves. They skitter intermittently on their curled
leaf-tips like desiccated arthropods over the
pavement. This sound is exaggerated in the
quietness of an October evening. It catches a
dreamer's attention at the edge of sleep, the sound
insinuating through the partially open bedroom
window. The dreamer mistakes it for the hesitant
footfalls of a prowler, or perhaps a cat, walking in the
leaves. These and other postulations equivocate at
the threshold of sleep as the dreamer submerges
once more into unconsciousness. The leaves
continue their erratic forays without purpose or
destination.

Barrie Nichol died in the autumn of 1988. For several weeks afterward the weather was unusually constant. Each afternoon large cumulus clouds mounted east of the city while, at the same time, a high, grey, uniform cloud-cover, thin enough to show the disk of the sun, spread over the sky. This layer of cloud subdued the light cast on the eastern cumulus banks and steeped their topography in a cool, grey summer light. The daily constancy of the clouds made each afternoon preternaturally similar, as if time had stopped and the same day was being replayed again and again.

These afternoons, with their neutral temperature, resonated in the absence Barrie's death had created. The unearthly permanence of the cloud banks made it seem that a new mountain range had risen east of the city. And yet, because all this structure and complexity was only water vapour in the atmosphere, floating islands sculpted by gravity and convection currents, the cloud banks became a paradigm of our own condition. We were like the clouds, sublime, marvellously detailed and ethereal all at once, mere convolutions of form with no permanence or substance. We were, as was everything around us, involutions of time and space. The world was a lucid, exquisitely complex, heartbreakingly beautiful, sad and strange illusion.

To awaken, dream, and then sleep again. We are thinking clouds.

NOVEMBER

November is the month of introspection,
of solitary walks to mysterious places.
It is a month of abandoned barns
and empty railway crossings.
Pale fields under pale skies.
November's transparent light
illuminates the dreaming landscape,
the blue autumnal mist.

In November the encounter
of winter and summer is
languorous and contemplative. They
cohabit gracefully, naturally,
as if they'd always
been together.

On unseasonably warm afternoons
the faded November sunlight
ignites a ghostly summer
in the branches of the willows.
A greenness where summer
still reigns.

November is the month of vistas.
The gaze is free-ranging,
unimpeded by dissembling foliage.
It is the month of ocular reverie.

Moss thrives in November.
Its greenness deepens
in a vernal expansion as it claims
what territory has been relinquished
by its perennial competitors.

November's wan light
is perfused with
the pensive satiety
that follows all celebration.
Green apples adorn
leafless branches like
forgotten ornaments
while a single November rose
blooms under winter's
neurological trees.

The first afternoon of winter
and the day glides,
and as it glides, unravels.
There is time to slip a decision
between the cycles, in the cusp
of time. The river
is not yet frozen. The cedars
green on its banks.

As weeks begin, as
seasons end, grant us a reprieve
within their term,
to delay an act, to act
in time. A symphony stirs
in another room. This
silence, this cool light.

The sunset, evening,
early morning, a time
for action, for inaction. The
morning stars condemn or ignore
our indecision. We abide
daily, listen for news
from ourselves, to glide, noiselessly
over the surface of some timepiece,
like an eclipse or turning
as polished aquamarine turns, spangled,

turns down, down, so listlessly
in this eternal autumn, this
winter solstice,
consumed.

She was sixty-five or seventy. She had had a stroke within the last year. She was clutching a chrome-plated cane that branched into four rubber-tipped prongs at its base. An older friend, possibly her sister, was fussing with shopping bags while she looked on. Although she leaned heavily on the cane, her head would sometimes jerk up and she would stare at certain people walking past whose pace was quicker than others in the crowd.

Perhaps these quick ones seemed to lurch towards her, for her eyes would widen. Perhaps their motion seemed a little uncanny, her belief and safety somehow taxed.

On that night like no other
when the moon first rose enthralled
from the amnion of the Pacific Ocean,
in the first bright inhuman flush
of moonlight,
I loved you there.
And when the new moon, impossibly huge,
with the sea still glistening on its sides,
ascended incomprehensibly
on the pedestal
of an immense tidal bulge,
I did not look away from you there.

Now, in the heartless perfection
of a winter afternoon
a single hawk hunts
over the snowy fields.
Ragged predator hovering
in the frozen wind.
And when evening gilds its hoary wings
I will wait for you.
For the moon rises again
a pale planet high
in the spectral air.
And when the fierce cold sparks
of winter stars are scattered
against the empty night
we will share a single
unbroken moment.

Love's awed cruelty spawned
our candid glance, this
opening we fell through. Axolotl.
We are salamanders
who've not yet shed
our gills. Axolotl.
Gasping in the
hard thin air of
destiny. How many
before me have sung
this intimate space?

This night beyond recall
is the heart of winter's
red darkness, words of love
rising like radio waves and
music, up into the deep overcast
of a winter night. Black
ink-wash. This house
the warm paradoxical heart
of an ice-age darkness.
Winter is the truest season,
its temperature closest
to that of interstellar space.

Beneath a starless sky
the farmhouse roof
glitters with hoarfrost.

On a distant ridge
the lights of other homes,
their private narratives
glowing in the darkness.
Tonight, spiralling deeper, deepest
into the soft void, the
impossible darkness, we
have a lover's tale to unravel.
Still, still night. The food
which nourishes us, hydromel. Hunter's rye.
By what new moons
have I known you?
In what darkness?
Surely now
something unknown
is passing between us.

Artifacts of Silence

*The water is clear as limpid air. They can see the tops
of great boulders a hundred feet down, shading to the
inky blackness that spreads beneath them like a velvet
tapestry, shifting occasionally as forms move under it.
No fish are visible in the clear areas near the surface,
and their presence can be inferred only by movements
and ripples of darkness at the margin of vision.*

*The lake spreads to the sky in every direction, a vast
round blue mirror with a line of red as the sun touches
the water. A light shock wave from the black depths,
indicating the passage of some large creature, rocks the
boat gently.*

WILLIAM BURROUGHS

This evening the desert wind
blows down the highway, stretches
fingers of sand across the asphalt.
We drive beneath a
night sky into the blank,
artificial darkness.
Our car is a chariot, is a blown
four-forty, a leaf, driven
by swamp gas
three-hundred million years old.
At the edge of the flats
there are mountains,
there are abandoned mines where
children toil.
Their lives are inconceivable
to themselves, as their suffering
is inconceivable to us.
And in the darkness
that illuminates this night
from the inside
the mountains are invisible,
locked out of the cones
our headlights make.

On the evening of
the last night you will ever
know, when the heavens
fall away and the planets

become magnified pictures of themselves,
like illustrations in a children's book,
there is a sky so blue it is inconceivable.
It is the darkness uncovered,
when night caves up
into a deeper midnight, a cobalt
so lost and intimate
that your heart fills
with dread and love.

And on this last night
your heart will form the shape
of a constellation and the sky
will ring with your music. The desert wind
will blow clear through you
and the mystery
of everything will be
absolutely still, transparent
at the centre
of a storm of glass.

But tonight we are merely adorned
with the instruments of our deaths.
Down the highway and through the night
we carry golden monkeys on our backs.
We drive
into the blank insulation
of all the sadness, all

the joys of life,
becoming a double crystal,
fire and ice.

Monkey-light.

It is our turn to know
the absolute, the pure
random.

The engineers who sound the whistle are neither happy nor sad – though the voice of the train, softened by the interceding air, has a thin, lonely sound. Distance makes it plaintive.

The whistle interrogates the emptiness around it. Its constant signature during our lives lends it an aural nostalgia and its voice is a summons to the greater world. For those who hear the whistle and for those who pause, but once, to hear the whistle's music, it is the sound of a passage that passes by.

The train whistle speaks of solitary travel. A melancholy refrain, a chord at once arbitrary and distinct, it calls us back. The train is hope of return, of destinations still awaiting.

When the world-lines converge
in the emptiness of sunlight
and causality thickens until
time stands still.

When you are
opened to contingency.

When you are so conscious that it skews
the balance of chance.

When the wind moves the leaves and
time slows. When time is made up of infinite,
discrete graduations,
      stroboscopic quanta,
second by second,
smaller even
than that.

Then the world opens.

Then the world rings
with destiny
under the strange music
of falling stars.

For eternity opens a divide so narrow
you cannot exist in it for the least portion of
a second.

And your schemes
must be drawn boldly
to pace the constant flux
of the world. Never the same
from second to second.
For ever and never.

In the absolute theatre of time
everything happens
at once and the world is immanent
with continuous form.

Tonight the wind blows through
all the worlds I have known and
through all the lives I have led.
The wind blows in the trees,
deeper into each.
The wind blows forever,
strains like something
endlessly departing.
Restless, impatient,
it races without burden.

The night wind implores me through walls,
claims me inside buildings.
The night wind is an empire
in exodus, a deliverance
beside the dark shapes of trees. Oaks
that wrestle the gusty twilight
under starry skies.

The wind takes
me in its giddy rush and
gathers me into a storm of longing,
rising on wings of darkness.
There is a music in the wind.
The thrum of guy wires,
of a thousand branches.
Muffled percussion
of banging doors, the
sibilous clamour of rushing leaves.

Above me the Milky Way
and leaping, striding, I am the
bloodrun of the atmosphere.
Racing with leaves and newspapers
down deserted streets,
over fields and playgrounds.
I pace the wind
through forests and beside highways.
Along oceans and rivers
the gale's mysterious, unspoken imperative
is a joyous delirium with
nothing at its end.

The miracle of your hair, obsidian mane
jet arborescence purple
                              by sunlight.
A sumerian flowerhead,
heavenly raiment of darkness.
The light of winter stars.

The miracle of your wrists
breathlessly spare, amber and milk articulate
with blue veins. Impossible stems
for the miracle of your hands.

The authority of your hands, candid
unafraid of earth
of flesh, the necessities of love.
Pale pink pillowed palms
your slender, gracile fingers,
their erotic benediction.

The miracle of your skin,
an ineluctable softness that extrapolates
your entire surface.

The miracle of your nipples
unearthly velvet. Honeyed spigots.

There is your brave nautical smile
afloat over your chin.

The miracle of your sex, heaven's gate
the interstice
of your thighs.
Night there.

And your legs
their long, almost ungainly grace.
The concord of your
lank, feral thighs.

Your feet
a celebration of earth and
all its miraculous parts,
triumph of muscle and tendon.
The slender sprawl of your toes
as you walk.

There is the miracle of you
in a moving taxi.
The languid authority of your carriage
an imperial choreography such
a convergent series of
graceful compensations.

Your back a facile treatise, vulnerable, curved.
Glissando of scapula and ribs. The
mitotic furrow of your spine.
The miracle of your hips, angel wings,

charmed protrusions asserting
the frank endowment of your sex.
Your breasts smooth full temples
outrageously adorned.

The miracle of your collarbones,
avian and delicate as your shoulders
their sharp dominion.

The miracle of your slightness,
your slender strength.
Our warrior of truth.

The miracle of your nose,
ineffable, angelic.

The miracle of your brow
clear and undaunted. Your neck
a heartbroken sanctuary.

The miracle of your eyes,
their green pluck. Feline and radiant.
The spirit I worship there.

Tonight this darkness,
this absence that we are,
is a night room
opening behind the stars.
We are children of the outer dark,
and in the agnostic lunar radiance
we have heard the shape
of falling stars. We have seen
angels in the windy summer night.
In the emptiness at
the surface of existence
we have seen angels like
hosts of entry, angels who
perforate everything
around the shape of the real.

We are those who love, we are
those whom fools thought
could move the world.
And the wind, supernatural,
like an abandoned votive ornament,
opens with emptiness the surface
of the night. And we who look on,
who merely regret, have
never loved nor thought
nor moved.

MONKEY LIGHT

In our lives we move deeper
through ourselves into each other
until our darkness, what is
unknown of ourselves to ourselves,
becomes a hardness, a closure.

It is then we resemble most
our monkey selves, with
our monkey language.
Inside the braided dance
of our lives, our solitary
poignancy becomes a gentle music
conspiring within us. Theme
opens through memory to
lock us into ourselves,
as if we could not parody
this tentative theatre.
As if we could not be happy on
this calm, this fair
day of our redemption.

We of the north
are masters of a net opened. Weirs
that sift the night wind.
We inhabit the treacherous surface
of electrical storms, we hide
in every miracle.
Above us the stars turn
as the earth turns but
it is a sad music, an overture
to exile. For we are tied to the world
by the shapes around us and
our hearts are broken
by such magnificent structure.

We live beneath a panoptic sky
impossibly deep, in which
the world floats
in the emptiness of the ideal.
Through the desert of our names
we are the frozen wind. For
we listen to the strange music
of the executioners. For
this darkness we return to
has no name.

Your parents have left you with relatives who live in
the country. It is the second morning of your visit
and you are beginning to feel homesick. You wander
alone beside a pond – the sunlight illuminates its
weedy bottom. The water is so clear that small fish
swimming over the sandy shallows seem to be
floating in the air. A breeze sets regular lines of small
waves on the far side of the pond. In the sky, white
clouds drift. Everything is iconic, and the light of
the sun is hollow, filling everything with emptiness,
a loneliness beyond consolation.

This single day in your life *was* your life. And your
afterlife is now, twenty years later, considering the
strange, intolerable miracle of that day. Two decades
later you have realized that that day, unremarkable
while experienced, was filled with cosmic
illumination.

Within that one day, a single representative
moment was frozen in a diorama, now installed in a
row along with such moments from other people's
lives, like mannequins in a store window. One of a
series of wax dioramas that lined the wall of a
basement gallery in an abandoned museum, water
dripping through the concrete roof.

That day had gestated invisibly in some recess of
your soul. It was the fulcrum of your life, the day you
were holographed by the universe. Twenty years

later it blooms into your awareness, a bright magnet for all the sadness, all the joys of your life. And now you understand that your greatest success will not be your adult achievements, your disappointments and tragedies, not the sum of your life, but that one day. That day of selfhood equal to the mystery of the universe.

M95ED is identical to our world, only you were never born. Your baby shoes were never purchased, your crib never filled. You never scraped your knee and cried as a six-year-old alone on a summer morning. Your voice did not ring out on this planet, nor did you walk upon its face. You never married the one you loved and you did not parent any children. No one needed you, no one plotted revenge against you. Your decline never came and you were never mourned. You had (simply, palely, thinly) never been.

Two figures walk along
the beach who, because
of their remarkable clothing,
expose and withdraw themselves
at the same time.

Two figures who walk
along the beach because
of their odd appearance
give the impression
of being foreign clothing.

Because of their odd
appearance they
give the impression
of being foreign
bodies on the beach.

Because they expose
and withdraw themselves
at a remarkable time
they deprive the scene
of easy comprehensibility.

Something mysterious and
unfathomable deprives the scene
of easy comprehensibility
and thereby closes it off from
the viewer in a singular way.

Something foreign deprives
the man lying on his back
of our gaze. He draws
our unfathomable wave to
his face, chest, and beach.

To the left we have a man
lying on his back with
legs stretched high and arms
tossed behind his head being
washed onto the beach by a wave.

To the icons he forms
something of a viewer
in a singular way and
thereby closes the scene
being washed onto the beach.

Two bulky wooden devices
float in the water.

Two bulky wooden devices
float in the water.

He forms something of a barrier
in front of the two women who,
like icons, look as though
they have been unselfconsciously
captured in a photograph.

59

He draws the two women
with their arms stretched
high and their heads
unselfconsciously exposed.

1.0 Language is like a hole for the future.

1.28 What I was talking about before I forgot what I was talking about.

1.29 All I need is a writing implement that will leave an indelible impression.

1.30 Impossible to lose anything in a two-dimensional universe.

1.81 Nothing is like this.

2.06 I am this way now.

2.53 Reality can't be duplicated.

2.56 I am, it is, we are.

2.92 All knowledge works back to an assumption.

3.08 Artifacts of silence.

Frozen in time,
her breasts framed
by the diagonals
of the white towel and
                  blue bathing suit,
she acquires
an almost ceremonial aura.
Her hands hover luminously
and animatedly
in front of the black water.

In this enraptured state
externals have become so insignificant
that she does not cover
her naked breasts.
The luminous
red-orange cloth on her head
and the yellow reflection
on her neck combine
to form a
secularized halo:
                  her radiant face is endowed
                  with an aura
                  of inviolable virginity.

The only difference between H26L3 and our own world is that during childhood every human on H26L3 is designated an executioner. The executioner, a master of stealth and disguise, is never far from his or her dependent. All executioners are instructed to shoot their wards with a high-powered rifle at the moment of the ward's greatest happiness. Like demented guardian angels the executioners save their charges from the humiliation and vagaries of old age and sickness.

The traffic in black-market depressants on H26L3 is enormous. Also, because orgasm is the most dangerous single killer, a panoply of non orgasmic varieties of sado-masochism flourishes.

One pair of lovers challenged their executioners for days with orgasm after orgasm, always promising the next would be better. It seems that the executioners knew the couple hadn't achieved their orgasmic potential and simply bided their time. But the man was accidentally shot first during what turned out to be a non-mutual orgasm. The woman survived for many years afterward and eventually committed suicide with heroin, cheating her own executioner.

A cold night. Cool,
sad summer wind blowing
through the porch screen.
Before me, in the dark forest,
the first angels appear.
They sing a world electrical
where appraisal
never found purchase.
A world where
the wind rushes, massless,
as if it were always
the sixth morning.
The luminous, cold sparks
of their music fall faintly as snow,
faintly as love abandoned
in a winter forest.

And through the facets
of this great nocturnal music
these seven angels pass
through my soul.
Seven angels pure
as a children's book
under the script of a vacant sky.

And while I stand alone
while the night caves in,

the angels dance electrical
as they merge into
the particularities of the world.

This is the word for the ideal.
    The ideal word for the idea.
This is the ideal world for the idea.
    In a word the ideal.

The word in an idea.
In an idea the word.
An idea in the word.
In the word an idea.

In a word the idea.

H10B7 is similar to our own world except that it orbits a rogue sun orphaned in intergalactic space. The near collision of two galaxies early in the evolution of the universe tore this planetary system and its sun from the arm of a spiral galaxy, stranding it in a region of the universe devoid of galaxies and stars. The nearest galaxy is so many millions of light-years distant the most powerful telescopes of world H10B7 cannot detect it.

Unlike our earth, which gathers new mass every day, H10B7 is dissipating. Because of its isolation in deep space its substance is evaporating directly into the interstellar void. H10B7 scientists have determined that their entire planetary system, including their sun, will vaporize into nothingness after millions of years. The origin and dimensions of the hungry void surrounding them is still a matter of intense speculation for H10B7 astronomers. Their cosmology is a poignant mixture of grandeur and loneliness arising directly from the overwhelming evidence that they are unique in the universe.

Except for the few points of light from other planets in the local system the night sky on H10B7 is utterly black. Walking home alone at night on H10B7 is a spookier, lonelier experience than walking alone at night on earth. The call of the whip-poor-will there is disturbing, like a rusty pump worked incessantly by a demonic, nocturnal vagrant, though the inhabitants of H10B7 do not find it so.

1.1   Practice differs from theory only when theory inadequately describes it.

1.24   An explanatory supposition based on principles independent of the phenomena to be explained

1.27   The signified stands to reason. (more or less)

2.2   I will harbour the roses in their concupiscence.

2.83   Random optical phenomena. Random optical

K37Y9 is populated by advanced beings who, through technological means, have divested themselves of their corporeal embodiment and their individuality. Existing as pure energy patterns, they have realized the dream of an immaterial, collective soul.

This goal took centuries to realize. Their first achievement had been technical immortality – souls encoded into pure energy waves. After having lived in this immaterial, deathless state for several centuries, they started to tire of their individual identities. They realized that identity bound them to a perpetual desert of existence and consequently they began to unite their individual souls into one central being.

Before they could join the group throng of unindividuated existence, however, they had to divest themselves of their personal memories. Reaching back into their lives they erased each memory forever, one memory at a time. This process was gradual, taking hundreds of years. Otherwise the cosmic nostalgia would have been too great. It would have broken their hearts.

Ultimately they distilled themselves down to one last memory. Perhaps an early childhood reminiscence, a walk in the sunlight holding their father's hand.

Then, this last memory erased, their individuality

disappeared. All the chains that bound the original soul to its past embodiment broke, and, weightless, it rose into the pulsing continuum of the group soul. A timeless, amnesiac radiance of pure being.